THE
Archive Photographs
SERIES

HEMEL HEMPSTEAD
A SECOND SELECTION

THE
Archive Photographs
SERIES
HEMEL HEMPSTEAD
A SECOND SELECTION

Compiled by
Eve Davis

CHALFORD

First published 1997
Copyright © Eve Davis, 1997

The Chalford Publishing Company
St Mary's Mill, Chalford,
Stroud, Gloucestershire, GL6 8NX

ISBN 0 7524 0745 7

Typesetting and origination by
The Chalford Publishing Company
Printed in Great Britain by
Redwood Books, Trowbridge

I dedicate this book to my dear family, and especially to my husband, Peter

Contents

Acknowledgements

I would like to thank the following people who have helped with photographs and information:

Den Bailey, John Ball, Miss Belt, Daphne Benton, Peter Benton, Mr & Mrs Brockett, Mr & Mrs Charge, Mrs J. Charman, Mrs Capel, Mrs E. Cooley, Marion Cowe, Miss Dale, Philip Earle, Mr & Mrs Elkins, Mr & Mrs Glover, May Greenaway, June Hollick, Mrs R. Hudson, Paul Jarvis, Mrs Jennings, Mr & Mrs Jordan, Mrs Lomax, Mrs P. Mason, Mr & Mrs Maynard, Mrs Meager, Mr & Mrs Minty, Mrs Marin, Ron Oldham, Joyce Ralph, Mrs B. Reynolds, Gladys Rolph, Betty Sangster, Maureen Stacey, Mike Stanyon (Heritage Store), Mr & Mrs J. Stevens, Jean Stopps, Mr & Mrs J. Selden, Mr Stubbington, Roger Sygrave, Mr & Mrs Thurlow, R. Tomkins, Pat Wilson, Hemel Hempstead Library, *Hemel Hempstead Gazette*, David Lavers of W.H. Lavers Ltd., County Record Office, Hertford. Special thanks to Mr Lawson who allowed me to use many photographs from his collection. To the staff of Kall Kwik, Peter and Len who have patiently dealt with my requests and obtained the best results from my old photographs. I have tried to include everyone who has lent me photographs and I am very sorry if I have inadvertently missed a name.

Introduction

Hemel Hempstead has for many years retained the atmosphere of a country town. Many residents today fondly remember the branch line railway from Boxmoor to Harpenden and the ribbon of small shops and houses that stretched along the length of Marlowes to the historic High Street.

1947 saw a turning point in Hemel Hempstead's history, when it was designated a 'New Town'. Without the help of old photographs it would often be difficult to remember which shops and buildings were there before 1947. Old maps of the area give a wonderful sense of the farms and fields that once existed, many of which would be lost to memory completely if some were not now used as street and road names. The Lockers, for instance, has a long history going back to 1552. Records show that it was bought in 1799 by Ebenezer Collett and turned into a gentleman's residence. Collett added several buildings, among which were a bakery, stables and coach house and extended the grounds to 107 acres so that they stretched to Crouchfield (now St John's Road). Collett School was named after him because it was built in the orchard of The Lockers. Ebenezer Collett disliked the idea of being buried in consecrated ground and demanded that, after his death, he should be buried as near his front door as possible at Lockers. His family were most upset at this and some time later moved him to the respectable spot of St Mary's Church.

Although Boxmoor is a district of Hemel Hempstead, residents have always felt it had its own identity. The moor stands in the midst of Boxmoor. This parcel of land was given to the earl of Leicester by Elizabeth I in the sixteenth century. Later, the land was given to the people 'for all time', and twelve Trustees were elected to look after the acres. Local people with 'pasture plaques' are still entitled to grazing rights and between May and November, horses, ponies and cows are allowed to graze on parts of the moor, under the supervision of the herdsmen employed by the Boxmoor Trust.

Over the years, many changes have been made to the area. The shopping area in St John's Road, known by residents simply as The Village, has unfortunately over the last few years lost much of its retail business, largely due to the change in people's shopping habits. The new bypass has claimed some of the ancient moorland, although, to compensate for this, new pieces of land have been purchased. Attractive features of the moor are the chestnut trees planted at the turn of the century and the new avenues planted for the coronation of King George V and King George VI.

Apart from the large firms like Dickinson's and Kent's, which employed many of the local people before the New Town Industrial Estate was established, there were many family businesses in Hemel Hempstead. The timber merchants, W.H. Lavers, are one such company who celebrated their centenary in 1968. William Henry Lavers began in London in a small way, with offices over a tea shop. He rented a small yard at Fishery Wharf and moved to larger premises in 1870 at Corner Hall, where the firm is to this day. Most of the important timber in the early days was brought from London by the canal on 50 ton barges which took three to four days to arrive. The business grew and prospered. The sawmill was replaced by modern machinery in 1914 but still worked by steam power. The fourth generation of the family still own and run the business.

Pemsel & Wilson also began a long time ago, in 1901. They had seen an advertisement in Hemel Hempstead for someone to start up a motor service between Boxmoor Station and the Town Centre, replacing the horsedrawn carriage. Arthur Pemsel and William Liley Wilson had vehicles available with drivers for private hire and organised outings. The early car engines were a constant source of trouble and if a vehicle broke down it was up to the driver to repair it. In 1914 Pemsel & Wilson became Ford agents. The name was changed to Boxmoor Motors in 1927 and the family connection was severed in 1961 when Ann and Rupert Wilson sold the business after sixty years. The motor business is now known as BMG Hemel Hempstead.

Henry Balderson was a dealer in coal and coke and an importer of wines and spirits. He became mayor in 1900 and also held other important positions in public life as director of both the gas and water companies. Balderson's Wharf in Two Waters Road later became well known for the aroma of lime juice which was stored in wooden barrels by a company called Roses who moved to Hemel Hempstead from London. The barrels were sprayed with water in warm weather to prevent them drying out. They closed in 1981 and on the site now stands a large DIY complex.

Arthur Harry Jarman, alderman, mayor and bailiff from 1933 to 1936, came from humble beginnings as one of seven children. He lived in Austin's Place, a small area behind the High Street and in his youth remembers seeing women strawplaiting outside their front doors. He had several jobs before he left school to help the family by earning a few pence. When employed at Dickinson's in Apsley he had to walk to work in all weathers and the working day began at 6 a.m. He was elected to the Borough Council in 1921 and continued until ill health forced him to retire from public life in 1952. Schools and hospitals were his special interest. Alderman Jarman's name lives on in the new complex at St Albans Road, called Jarmans Field.

William Crook was a well-known schoolmaster, magistrate and local historian who devoted many years to recording the town's past. He became mayor in 1953 and was made a Freeman of the Borough in 1965. He was often seen cycling around town on his old 'sit up and beg' bicycle. WGS, as he was known, was a director of the Hemel Hempstead Building Society, which was taken over by Birmingham Midshires. The building has been converted into a tastefully decorated pub and restaurant called The Society Arms.

I hope that my *Hemel Hempstead: a Second Selection*, will both bring back memories for those who knew the town as it was and interest newcomers. This book of photographs is another small contribution to local history and a way of preserving the memories that could so easily be lost to future generations.

One
Marlowes and High Street

This engraving of William Ginger's Villa, now known as The Bury, is dated 1796. Earlier buildings and grounds date back to the fifteenth century and were once in the possession of Richard Combe and his descendants. The house has undergone many changes and is now the headquarters of the Divisional Education Office and the Register Office.

View from the top of the railway bridge looking along Marlowes, 1950s. The row of small cottages on the left were the first to be demolished when the road was widened. The Waggon & Horses pub on the far left was demolished many years later, in 1989. A wide variety of shops catering for every need once extended along Marlowes.

Reg Moore taking a little time off work from his shoe shop, begun by his father Francis in 1912. The Waggon & Horses on the other side of the road was then still in place. Mr Moore moved to St John's Road, Boxmoor, in the 1950s.

The demolition of the railway bridge that spanned Marlowes for almost 100 years took place in July 1960. Road widening had already taken place and the new Co-op building can be seen through the arches.

Construction of BP House buildings which stretched from the Leighton Buzzard Road to McAlpines at the botton of St Albans Road, July 1962. Later in 1988/9 this too had to be demolished because it became unsafe. The new shops in Marlowes can be seen in the distance.

Some of the many little shops people will remember near the railway bridge in Marlowes: Moore's, Hemming's, Edmund's, Fortnum's, Garment's, Smith's and Harris's. This view is possibly from the early 1920s.

Early photograph of Marlowes 1905 with Edmunds Place on the left next to E. Keen the butchers. Cossor's, Monk's, Cannon's and Frith's were the names of some of the shops on the other side of the road. Traffic was very light and life more leisurely then.

Further along Marlowes was The Henry VIII pub and next to it was the Flower Box and Gordon Phillips & Maud Kershaw, ladies outfitters. This is the area where Bank Court now stands. The large building in the distance is the Luxor Cinema in the 1930s.

Marlowes, looking back towards The Plough at Moor End. On the left-hand-side is Viney's stationers and post office, Heads sweet shop, Beaven cycles, the National and Provincial Bank, Halfway House, Humphreys and Hendersons. They all traded here before the first re-development in the 1950s.

This unusual and impressive house was situated opposite the Luxor in Marlowes. It is thought to have been occupied by the Clark family who had a bakery at the bottom of the High Street. The Sygrave family also lived there around 1900/10 and it was later Havenden's the chiropodist. This and other houses were demolished to make way for redevelopment in the 1950s.

Boy's Brigade, marching along Marlowes towards Bridge Street. The Luxor Cinema and Saunders Garage were familiar landmarks. Note the telegraph poles and absence of road markings.

The new post office was opened in 1937 and replaced the smaller one in Alexandra Road. This view shows the many large trees that still existed along Marlowes in the 1930s. This classic building was demolished in July 1985 and a new glass structure built next door.

New Post Office, Hemel Hempstead.

View from the top of the multi-storey car park, 1960s. The post office is on the far left, next to the gas showrooms and electricity offices. The market square was by this time well established after its move from the old part of the high street. Pyle & Thomson was the electrical shop on the corner in the foreground.

This family plumbing, decorating and furnishing business was near a row of shops in Hospital Lane (now Hillfield Road). The style of the baby carriage dates this photograph as around 1910.

An old view of Marlowes looking north, c. 1900. This photograph was taken well before the road was surfaced and the shops and houses built in between the gaps. Quite a few of the large elegant houses are still standing, although they are now no longer private homes, but estate agents, solicitors and building societies.

Marlowes, at the junction of Combe Street. The Odeon was completed in 1960 and is now a bingo hall. Old buildings have been cleared to make way for the Pavilion and health centre. Just beyond are the Co-op buildings and the Princess theatre. Both the chimney of the water works and the spire of St Mary's stand out on the skyline.

A closer view of the Co-op, then called Berkhamsted & District Co-operative Society, 1950s. Next door is the Princess cinema which opened in December 1912, showing silent films seven days a week. Just in view is Red Tiles cafe.

On the other side of the road was Miss Fodens Nursery, heavily covered in ivy and bushes. The business later became Brown & Merry estate agents. The buildings were cleared and the site is now a Jewish residential home for the elderly.

Entrance to Gadebridge Park. The mock Tudor buildings were known as the Broadway. The first part used to be the old fire station until it moved to new premises in Alexandra Road in 1937. This picture shows that it was also for a while the London Transport Country Buses office, situated only a short distance from where the buses used to line up along Bury Road. Several businesses, including a sub-post office and Pearl Assurance insurance company, had premises there.

An early view of the High Street, *c*. 1900. A few of the twenty-four pubs along the street include the White Hart and the Rose & Crown, whose signs are visible in this picture. George Day, the stationers, printers and newsagents had windows full of merchandise. W.H. Smith also had a shop a few yards away. The Town Hall's domed top and weathervane were later removed.

Upper High Street, around 1955. George Rolph was one of the many shops well remembered for selling furniture and drapery. Next door was the Sun Inn. Chennells, the grocer and Gower, the ironmongers, also had premises in this area. 'Down the dip' on the right were more pubs and shops including Herbert East, outfitter. This part of town was made famous when the TV series *Pie in the Sky* was filmed here.

Aerial view of the top end of town. St Mary's Church is very prominent, as is The Bury, a large
white house with a very long history. Bury Mill is at the bottom of the photograph. Dacorum
College and grounds were built on a large area in between Alma Road and Bury Road. The large
open space became Gadebridge Park.

Two
Around the Town

Elegant front door and porch of Lockers, Bury Hill. This has seen many changes since it was occupied by Francis King, a JP and bailiff in 1677. It has since been converted into flats.

Water End bridge dates from the nineteenth century, but looks older. This picturesque landmark is forced to cope with twentieth-century traffic.

A tranquil view of the Golden Parsonage near Gaddesden Row, home of the Halsey family for many generations. The present building dates from 1706 and became a boy's school in 1912. It became the home of the Halsey family again in 1950 and its present occupants are Mr and Mrs Nicholas Halsey, who moved there in 1980.

Gaddesden Place, built by James Wyatt in 1770 and renovated by Sir Frederick Halsey, MP for West Herts, between 1874 and 1906. It was very badly damaged by fire in 1905. The Halsey family have been connected with this area since the fifteenth century.

Skating at Gaddesden Hall Farm, winter 1905.

True Blue Inn, Cupid Green, was situated near the junction of Redbourn Road and St Agnell's Lane. Some locals think the name came about because the wooden parts were painted bright blue. The licensee Thomas Roots is standing in one doorway, with his wife and son in the other. The stables and sheds were still there in the late '60s. This photograph was taken around 1907.

Stables and buildings in the 1960s, before they were demolished to make way for wider roads.

The True Blue later became a private home, although the name of the gate served as a reminder of its former identity. A porch was added, and the existence of old doorways are revealed on the brickwork around the ground floor windows.

A very early photograph of Hammerfield taken by a local photographer, J.H. Sadler, who was in business here in 1904. This picture recalls a time before buildings had started to crop up between the pine trees.

Row of white brick houses in Glenview Gardens, 1905. People used to meet at number 5, at the home of Mr E. Styles, to pray, before St Francis Church was built in 1908. This postcard, dated 7 March 1905, was written with the intention of helping someone find a home in the district.

Frederick Breed & Sons, printers, had premises at 48 Alexandra Road between 1906 and 1937, according to Kelly's directories. It's a pity the notices on the boards cannot be clearly read.

Bridge Street, taken from Cemetery Hill at the junction with Cotterells. Marlowes is in the distance. These buildings were all demolished when redevelopment took place in the '50s. Now we have busy roads, a pedestrian crossing over the Leighton Buzzard road and car parks instead.

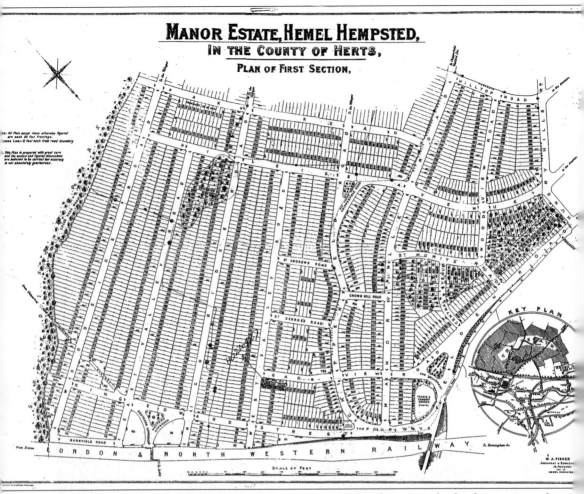

Plans for the proposed building of the Manor Estate, 1903. This was only the first section of what seems to be an enormous project. The circular key plan gives some idea of how far the whole estate was intended to spread.

This photograph, dating from the early 1930s, shows a different section of the planned Manor Estate, showing a mixture of bungalows and houses. This view differs from the original plan of 1903, in which there were 20 ft frontages for each plot.

A picture of Belswains Lane, possibly before 1900. Locals still call Belswains the 'Back Lanes'.

Cox Pond Farm, *c*. 1911. The farm was at this time owned by Fred and Polly Dell. When it was later demolished to make way for redevelopment, it was taken down brick by brick and moved to Harpenden Common.

HOBLETTS MANOR TO BE DEMOLISHED

This picturesque old house at Adeyfield—Hobletts Manor—is soon to be demolished to make way for new development. The land has been leased by the New Towns Commission to C. T. Crouch Ltd., who propose to build 29 three- and four-bedroomed detached houses on the site. The builders, who are clients of Brown & Merry, the Hemel Hempstead Estate Agents, expect the first houses to be completed by August or September. They will cost from £5,900 to £6,425 leasehold, and are offered for sale from today (Friday). The manor house, previously the home of Brig. G. B. S. Hindley, general manager of the former Development Corporation, had been converted from two Elizabethan cottages.

Hobletts Manor, Adeyfield, was converted from two Elizabethan cottages. According to the Ordnance Survey Map of 1898 it was then known as Hoblets Orchard. The old house was demolished in the 1960s.

Alford & Alder's new factory, built on the corner of Maylands Avenue and Maxted Road in the early 1950s. The site covered 5 acres. The firm began by building horse-drawn carriages in London in 1818 and have been associated with the motor industry since the 1900s. The company's final years were spent producing steering units for cars, trucks and buses. The factory closed down in 1980/1.

Maylands Avenue, one of the newest roads in the Industrial Estate. The first building on the left, Multicore Solders, moved to Hemel Hempstead from Slough in 1952 and was at the Wood Lane End site from 1984.

New Town development at Warners End, 1953. In this aerial view, we can see the base being prepared for the Stoneycroft shops. The large parkland area enclosed by trees is part of the Northridge Estate, owned by Nathaniel Micklem. Northridge Farm stands nearby. The curved road stretching away into the distance is Boxted Road leading to Potten End. Long Chaulden and Northridge Way are also visible.

Three
Apsley

Apsley Mills, *c.* 1920. This picture was taken before new 'departments' replaced the Apsley Vicarage and the Salmon Meadow. In the days before heavy traffic, children played with hoops and balls in the road.

Two Waters, Apsley End and the confluence of the Bulbourne and Gade rivers. Swans and other aquatic birds were often seen nesting here. The Bell Inn is a well established building dating back to the sixteenth century.

Apsley Top Lock. The canal was an important part of Apsley's industry and was used for carrying waste paper, coal and timber. In the distance is the Albion Bridge and Ebberns Road.

London Road, Apsley. The White Lion pub and the post office stood on the corner of White Lion Street. There was also McKay's barbers and tobacconists, Eastman's butchers shop, Patterson's drapery, Huxley's menswear, Dr Young's surgery, Simmond's and Buckle's greengrocers, Bishops' grocers, Thurlow's newsagents, Stratford shoes, Smart's chemist and G.B. Kent brush manufactory.

Storey Street, Apsley, with the junction of London Road, c. 1910. The corner shop has, in its time, been a shoe maker, fish shop and carpet shop. The Spotted Bull opposite has changed, but is still recognisable. The main road is always full of traffic, despite the new bypass.

The Albion, Durrants Hill Road, is marked on the tithe map of 1836 as a cottage, garden and wharf. The Albion stabled those horses which worked on the canal. In 1851, James Turnham was the beer seller and in 1891, A. Simpson was the landlord. Later landlords included Charlie Sexton (1912/37) and John Crawley. The present landlord is Paul Jarvis.

Two Waters Sunday School outing to Totternhoe Knoll, 1908. This event involved people of all ages, from babies and children to adults.

Miss Dorothy Mabel Tyers outside her home in Weymouth Street, Apsley, *c.* 1908. Miss Tyers had a long teaching career, first at Two Waters School and then the old Central School, before going on to Corner Hall. She was also a talented musician and played for the Watford Philharmonic Society and the Hemel Hempstead Operatic and Dramatic Society.

Children playing in Weymouth Street, Apsley, *c.* 1904. St Mary's church spire can be seen in the distance.

Photo by C. A. Patterson

The Church of Saint Mary
Apsley End
Herts

Front cover of a book, published in 1932, celebrating over sixty years of St Mary, Apsley End.

The church of St Mary has six bells cast by Mears & Stainbank of Whitechapel Bell Foundry, London. The bell ringers pose with their handbells in this picture of 1932. Standing, left to right: E. Picton, C. Henley (captain), H. Rogers, F. Tompkins. Sitting, left to right: A. Good, R. Bruce (secretary), W. Feasey.

G.B. Kent & Sons football team, after having just won 'The Uncle's Cup', 1908. Very proudly displayed on the board are the words: 'Kent's Best British Brushes'. The firm was established in London in 1777 and moved to Apsley at the turn of the century.

North End Time Office dwarfed by the Card and Board Department, 1935. The small buildings on the far right were the parish rooms of St Mary's.

Group of John Dickinson employees waiting outside the main entrance. Beyond the trees was 'The Cottage', part of the original mill which later contained a board room, director's dining rooms and first-aid room.

Programme advertising a reunion dinner for old Apsley colleagues held in the Guildhouse, 24 March, 1939. It shows the carved wooden fireplace of Shendish House built in 1854-6 which became a clubhouse and headquarters of the Guild of Sport for John Dickinson employees in 1937.

FIREPLACE IN THE MAIN HALL OF SHENDISH HOUSE

A charabanc outing for John Dickinson employees to the popular Bricket Wood, 1920s. Edie and Gladys Bradley and W.J. Sygrave are the only named passengers.

Abbot's Hill, built in 1836 by John Dickinson. He insisted that, like his workmen's cottages, it only have one door onto the outside world. It passed out of John Dickinson's family and in 1912 became a private school, which it still is today.

Red Lion Inn, near the railway bridge and Rucklers Lane, c. 1910. This was a popular stopping place for liquid refreshment and a little light entertainment.

Four

Boxmoor

Balderson's Bridge, or the High Bridge, in Two Waters Road, 1923. The bridge was built when the canal became an important means for transporting heavy goods, such as coal from the midlands to London, in the 1790s. It was named after Henry Balderson, who was a dealer in coal, corn and stone and an importer of wines and who leased the nearby wharf. Roses lime juice arrived in 1946 and stayed until the 1980s. It is now the site of B & Q, the DIY specialists.

Canal Cottage 101, at lock 62, Grand Union Canal. The cottage may date from as early as 1832. The lock-keeper and his family grouped by the front door look serious and this photograph may have been taken on an important occasion.

Close-up of the lock-keeper, his wife and son at the front door of the cottage. The date 1905 above the door may refer to the time that repairs took place to the cottage. In the 1930s a family named Climpson lived here, but the cottage became empty in the late 1940s. It has been modernised since and is occupied today.

RAILWAY STATION, BOXMOOR.

Card postmarked July 1904. A view from Fishery Lock across the moor towards Boxmoor station. The large white house is the Railway Hotel, or 'The Tavern'. Railway workers cottages and the station can be seen through the trees.

Brook and Moor, Boxmoor.

Children enjoying paddling in the River Bulbourne alongside the canal. Although this area later had a brick edging, the natural river bed remained unchanged.

The first photograph of Boxmoor signal box sheds and sidings is taken from Roughdown Avenue, c. 1950. The garden gate in the foreground led to the home of George Wilkes, Wembley Lions speedway rider. The second snapshot is a close-up of the signal box and was taken in the days when the controls were manually operated and steam trains were run by the LMS.

Cows grazing on the moor in the days before the grassy area was fenced. The telegraph poles follow the line of the canal. Foster's saw mills and chimney are visible on the right hand side. The Fishery Inn and the old iron bridge across the canal help to date the photograph, as an attractive balustrade bridge was completed in 1927.

The demolition of the sawmills belonging to Fosters in Kingsland Road, August 1969. The sawmills were an important part of Boxmoor village life for many years and employed many local people. A serious fire hastened the end of the mills and today flats cover this site, now known as River Park.

Sebright Road, Boxmoor, named after Sir John Sebright, who built an infirmary for Hemel Hempstead in 1831, which later became known as Cheere House. The houses were built by the Gower Brothers, whose nameboard is displayed on the wall of the first house. These houses remain unchanged today.

St John's Road, Boxmoor, c. 1929. Mr W.H. Hicks once kept a fish shop here. His mother moved into a double-fronted shop opposite, converted from a house by Mr Fred Gower. The flint cottages on either side of the road have since been modernised, but otherwise remain intact. Weston's fish shop is still going strong, but is now under new management.

Village shops, *c.* 1906. Smiths and W.H. Gale were the two shops on the left hand side by the raised paving. Farm and dairy can be seen at the junction of Anchor Lane and St John's Road. The Three Blackbirds pub can be seen just beyond. Emma Hollicks, newsagents and tobacconists, were also house furnishers and barbers. Hollicks had family connections with the watercress industry and skips of local cress were usually on sale outside.

St John's Road, looking back towards the village. The Catholic church of St Mary and St Joseph officially opened in 1898 and this view was taken before the church was enlarged and the entrance moved around the corner. The Three Blackbirds is one of the town's oldest public houses, and dates from around 1760. It has been updated several times and on the last occasion an old bakers oven was discovered. A pavement was constructed on the other side of the road in the 1960s.

The Post Office, Boxmoor

The new post office opened in 1906, replacing the one in the drapers and wool shop in St Johns Road. In this picture, family and staff stand proudly outside the new, larger premises. Behind it stood the post office rooms, an important sorting office convenient for the railway station nearby. The office is still trading and much in demand, the rooms behind now belonging to a Montessori nursery school. On this corner of Horsecroft Road is Foster Road leading to the saw mills.

This little corner shop was a general grocers for many years. In 1933 it was the home of Horace Crawley. It was previously known as Rastells and, between 1900/10, was occupied by the Thorne family. It has also been a craft shop.

Horsecroft road in the 1930s looks deserted by today's standards. On closer inspection a few Union Jacks can be seen: could it be Empire Day or a royal event? The houses varied in style, as they were built at different times. In the early days, people were encouraged to buy a property and have the benefit of free rail travel.

The Grapes public house in Green End Road, *c.* 1937. The flags outside suggest it may be for the coronation of George VI. The landlord in the 1930s was Augustus Hill. Other neighbours were 'Lally' Pipkin and 'Granny' Ranscombes, who used to sell sweets to the local children. Most of these buildings were demolished to make way for a car park for the Grapes.

Boxmoor House was built in the 1850s for a London surgeon Thomas Davis. In the 1870s it became the home of revd. James Blackwood and his wife Alicia, who hosted large mission gatherings when she was in her 90s. It became a convalescent home for soldiers in the First World War, then changed again to a home for 'Imbecile Children of Gentle Folk'. The house was bought by Hertfordshire County Council in 1942 and is now known as Boxmoor House School.

Cardy House, Boxmoor, 1961. One of the large elegant houses built in the area of Gravel Hill Terrace. In the 1930s the house was owned by Ald. C.E. Stevenson.

Cardy House, Little Orchard, showing masses of daffodils in the spring. The drive leading to the house is on the right hand side.

"Churchill" Hemel Hempstead.   129958

The grounds of Churchill House in St John's Road opposite St John's Church. The house was previously known as The Heath and built in 1830. Many people remember the name of Mitchell-Innes who lived there for many years and had very close connections with the church. The house was sold to the borough in 1934, used for family welfare clinics until the early 1960s, then demolished to make way for the Dacorum Sports Centre.

Boxmoor Hall was built for the community in 1890 and designed in the Flemish style. It was once a court house and a venue for many important public meetings.

Five
Schooldays

Teachers of Two Waters Sunday School dressed in their best for an outing to Totternhoe, *c.* 1906. Only a few names are known: Mr Goodman (far left), Mr Coleman (centre) and Mr G. Hughes, superintendant (far right).

Aerial view of St Nicholas House School showing the extensive grounds and school buildings. It was formerly known as 'The Hollies' and owned by the Marnham family.

St Nicholas House School was founded by two sisters by the name of Brown, in Stanmore, London, in 1923, and was moved to Hertfordshire in 1944 because of the bombing during the Second World War. Miss Muriel Clegg served as headmistress here for almost twenty years. The school moved to join Abbots Hill School in 1969.

No trace of this school can be found on maps of the Lockers area, but it is believed to have been where Pinewood Gardens is now. St Antoine's was a small, private, primary school in the 1950s.

St Johns Hall, 1947. This private school occupied part of St Johns Hall. Miss Cooper and Miss Smith were the teachers at this time and Richard Cooper, Michael Hayter, Dickon Cranswick and Diane Slatter are among the children pictured here.

St John's Boys School, Boxmoor, *c.* 1910. Mr W. Thorne is in the second row from the front, fifth from the left. The headmaster in this era was Mr F. St John Badcock.

Mr C. Jenkins, school master at St Johns School, with the football team of 1937. He served at the school for thirty-two years, from 1907 and died in 1939.

May Day celebrations at Boxmoor Infants School, Cowper Road, 1930s. Henry Charge is the one in the front row on the left with one sock up and one down. Parents look on behind the school railings.

Hemel Hempstead Grammar School VI Form, Summer 1951. Back row, left to right: Bryan Sparrow, -?-, Colin Dixon, Bernard Bloom, Stan Miller, David Wallis, Bryan Syms, -?-, -?-, John Latchford, Michael Putnam. Centre, left to right: Rhoda Atkins, Ann Knight, Mary Tutt, Joyce Walmsley. Front row, left to right: Marion Cowe, Muriel Holliday, Brenda Wright, Miss Duncan, Mr M. Evans, Connie Terry, Pamela Fancourt, Ishbel Dornan.

Piccotts End School, built in 1877 and enlarged in 1906. It served the local children until 1939, when the Second World War resulted in its closure. This photograph shows its rural setting.

Piccotts End school children, *c.* 1932. Standing, are: Mary Ball, Daphne Ward, Sylvia Pearman, Betty Gammons, Thora Dennis. Kneeling, are: Betty Ludlow, Betty Minty, Dorothy Collier, Stella Gardener, Barbara Simmonds and Nora Crane.

A very early photograph of George Street School football team, 1895. It was taken in a photographer's studio and it must have been an ordeal to keep still.

George Street school football team around 1917. The boy on the far left is Roland Scott and the boy in front with the ball is Bertie Payne. The games master was J.J. Eyre.

Two Waters School, July 1936. Back row, left to right: John Bonaker, Roy Jackson, Lionel Geary, Brian Longbottom, Sheila Bradshaw, Alec Mason, Jean Baxter, Donald Kibble. Front row, left to right: Ian McGregor, Ruth Huxley, Alan Gover, Gillian Hill, Betty Hall.

Children outside the Primitive Methodist Chapel, Boxmoor, 1950s. Those pictured include Janet Smith, Sheila Mead, Stephen Lomax, Joan Mead, Ivor and Philida Cleveland, Kenny and Shirley Frost, the Dunn family, Noreen Mead, Dick Crew, the Gillan family, Paul Jones, Graham Waller, Janet Pugh and the Findley family.

Chaulden Hall, a venue for Sunday School meetings, Harvest Festival 1956. On the platform was John Seddon, Mr Williamson, a local preacher and organist, Mr E. Brown, superintendent. Among the children pictured are: Robert and Tyrone Adams, Shirley, Kenneth and Janet Frost, Paul Jones, Sheila and Doreen Mead, Maureen Wildman, Helen Lomax and the Findley family.

Hemel Hempstead Grammar School, Old Scholars Hockey Team. Back row, left to right: Barbara Simmonds, Ada Hancock, Peggy Pollard, Edna Cutler, -?-, -?-. Front row, left to right: -?-, -?-, Sylvia Hollick, ? Goodman, Margaret ?.

Queen Street School, *c.* 1922. Miss Thurnham was the headmistress. Some of the children took part in a play called *Old Dame*. Front row, left to right: Bill Parr, Bill Sygrave, -?-, Dolly Harris, -?-, -?-, -?-, Les Foster, -?-, -?-, Ted Parr. Standing: Miss Thurnham, -?-, Nellie Vaughan, George Halsey, Bill Collier.

Central School pupils relaxing after a ramble and picnic, 1937.

Corner Hall boys presenting *A Midsummer Nights Dream*, 1941/2. Back row: Mrs Cameron (Titania), ? Geary (Bottom), -?- (Oberon). Next row: Stella Griffiths, Marie Delamuro, Diana Holt, Doreen Stacey, Janice Preston, Gwen Belden, -?- (Puck). Second row: Betty Purseglove, Doreen Bygrot, ? Scott, Stan Tricker, Pat Venables (fairy), Lionel Killick, Colin Woods, John Tubby. Front row: Betty Robinson, ? Brown, -?-, -?-, -?-, Peter Gatehouse, Bob Priestnal, ? Bayliss, Mel Hopla.

Crabtree Lane Secondary School for Girls, the Prefects Summer, 1949. Back row, left to right: Sheila Parkins, John Hosier, Eileen Charge, Marjorie Palmer, Josephine Grayson, Denise Robinson, Jean Gower. Front row: Stella Hoar, Jean Rabbatts, Joan Daniels, Doreen Cook (Head Girl), Evelyn Hobbs, Ann Croker, Margaret Oakley.

Six
Work and Transport

Haymaking at Cox Pond Farm in the days before mechanisation. Around 1911 it was owned by Fred and Polly Dell.

This trade horse and cart owned by the Hemel Hempstead Co-operative Society won third prize at a horse show in Gadebridge Park on August Bank Holiday, 1911.

The local baker, A.W. Scott, who had premises behind buildings in Fensoms Alley, c. 1920. Mr Hannel is the one holding the horse's reins. The horse's name was Dolly.

Another one of the many small bakers in the district. The cart is piled high with bread and is almost defying gravity. There seem to have been no hygiene regulations about bread being left uncovered in the early years of this century.

BSA motorbike and sidecar owned by Fred Radford, who had a dairy business off Queen Street (Queensway) and lived in Half Moon Yard, which is now the Day Centre. He married a Miss Howe and moved into Great Road. He was a most popular milkman in the area and changed his horse and cart for a more modern form of transport in the 1930s.

Postman Tommy Preston delivering the mail in a heavy fall of snow, December 1926. He sadly lost his wife when a bomb fell on his house at 33 Astley Road in 1940.

This forge was run by the Hemmings family and, according to Kelly's, occupied premises at 5 Cotterells from 1906 to 1937. The place is now a petrol station.

W.H. Lavers & Sons, timber merchants at Corner Hall Wharf, established in 1870. The soft wood is stacked in open piles and allowed to season. The man on the far right is presumed to be W.H. Lavers himself.

Ebberns Road, Apsley, cutting chestnut pailings. The man on the right is Mr Hall. John Dickinson's factory chimneys are in the background.

One of the two butchers who owned premises and a slaughterhouse in St John's Road, Boxmoor. This picture shows the staff outside the shop, *c.* 1927. The year before, W. Charman took over from J. Loosley. Miss Speed, the cashier, is second from the left, next to Mr Charman and Herb Owen is in the striped apron on the right of the photograph.

Further along was another family butchers run by Philip Earle and his wife Sheila who served in the cooked meats shop and behind the cash desk. From 1906 to the 1920s the trading name was Fulks, and in the 1930s it became Lovetts. The picture shows Philip and his assistant Chris in the last week before closure in June 1988.

Local girl, Nellie Dolt, working at her paper-folding machine.

C. Brice, coal merchant, had premises on the London Road, near Boxmoor Station. The firm won first prize in the Hospital Parade, in 1931. Mr George Minter, the driver, started work for the firm when he was 18 years old and stayed until the business closed, thirty-seven years later. This photograph was taken in Salmon Meadow, Apsley.

Advertising board for Pemsel & Wilson, automobile engineers who had a garage, workshop and offices in Boxmoor. The business was founded in 1901.

Extensive line-up of Ford Cars in a competition at Pemsel & Wilson's premises on the London Road. The goods yard of Boxmoor station is in the background.

Staff and workers of Pemsel & Wilson, 1920s. Top left, left to right: Collard, Nobby Batchelor, Butler (foreman), Davies. Second row, left to right: Major Pipkin, Flack, Bunce, Gill, petrol boy. Standing, left to right: -?-, Burchell, William L. Wilson, Arthur Pemsel, Attfield. Front row, left to right: Ann Wilson, -?-, sales girl, Dutton, sales rep for Vigzol motor oil.

Large advertisement for West Herts Hospital Wireless Fund. The public are being asked for their donations, to go towards buying a wireless and headphones for hospital patients.

The Daimler had a wagonette type body, canopy and curtains and could seat up to eight people. This model was called 'Shamrock'.

The Wilson family, picnicing in the country, 1902. Grandma is cautiously staying under cover.

Early photograph of W.W. Saunders' premises near Bridge Street in Marlowes. The family home was next door to the garage. The business was enlarged and modernised, and moved to Moor End when redevelopment took place in the early 1950s. Its name was then changed to Shaw & Kilburn.

Ladies and children's hairdresser at no. 17 Alexandra Road, owned by Betty Sangster. Half of the premises were previously owned by F. Barrett Gardiner, a well known photographer until his retirement in 1952. Next door was the fire station.

Photograph of William Brock, a descendant of John Brock, founder of Brocks Fireworks. The factory moved to Hemel Hempstead from London in the 1930s, because they could build many small units here and store in safety all the chemicals needed to make the fireworks.

BROCK'S SET THE STANDARD

These pictures from the 1880's show Brock's employees making various fireworks using wooden and brass tools—note too the legally required overboots in the rocket charging scene. C. T. BROCK (1843–1881) played a major role in the drafting of the Explosives Act of 1875 which continues to impose considerably more rigorous conditions on UK manufacturers than similar legislation in other countries, both East and West.

MAKING CRACKERS

CHARGING HEAVY ROCKETS

CHARGING SHELLS

In the 1980's many processes are still carried out by hand using similar tools and procedures to those seen in these pictures but the pioneering by BROCK'S of new materials and designs ensures continuing improvements in quality and performance.

MAKING CATHERINE WHEELS

Reproduction post-card showing some of the stages in making fireworks for Brocks in the 1880s.

Seven
People and Places

Young soldiers in the First World War, playing music while off duty. Some of these lads were in the third Boxmoor Boy Scouts Troop. Only one name is known, that of Stan Baines.

Soldiers billeted at what later became Tillingbourne Hay in Gravel Hill Terrace, cleaning out the stables in 1914.

View of the stables at Tillingbourne Hay, *c.* 1960. They were later converted into living apartments. The house was occupied by the Brock family before they moved to Woodhall Farm.

Southern aspect of Cardy House, *c.* 1926, showing the Aldenham Harriers Hunt. Alderman C.E. Stevenson was the owner of Cardy House and Master of the Harriers. The huntsmen wore green and yellow (not hunting pink) coats, and white breeches.

Employees of John Dickinson getting ready for a wagonnette outing. Hats and pale dresses were the order of the day, *c.* 1910.

Presentation taking place at The Cottage, Apsley, *c.* 1942. The Cottage was the original part of Apsley Mills and around the late 1920s was extended to provide a new board room, visitors dining rooms and nurses first-aid room. Rosemary Allen and Mrs Beck the canteen manageress are featured here.

The Dickinson Team, who won the Linotype Shield on 18 June 1910. The event was a 'two miles flat interteam race' and the winners were presented with gold medals.

Hemel Hempstead Grammar School, Form VL, Summer 1950. Back row, left to right: Mary Tutt, Brenda Martin, Marjorie Farley, Rita Lawrence, Pam Weaver, Janet Lee, Christine Baxter, Joyce Williams, Joyce Trend, David Tyler, Shirley Draper, Joan Dimmock, Keith Johnson. Middle row, left to right: Joan Banfield, Margaret Stockman, Angela Matthews, Olive Mason, Mr E. Evans, Doris Wright, Ann Flory, Pam Walsingham, Phyllis Reading. Front row, left to right: Ann Knight, Marion Cowe, Roger Coleman, Keith Parrott, Michael Elliott, James Elborn.

May 1969, the mayoress, Mrs Hannam-Clark, took part in welcoming the Czechoslovakian ambassador, Dr. Miloslau Rusek, to International Week: eight days of drama, music and dance. The children taking part in the celebrations came from Maylands Infant School, where Mrs Hannam-Clark was Headmistress.

Hemel Hempstead Food Office staff during 1940/5. Unfortunately, only the surnames are known. Back row: Waghorn, Wynn, Hawten, O'Dell, Sheffield. Second row: -?-, Swift, Wardley, Charman, Toomey, Wilkes, Bennett, Lovesay, Crick, Nicholls. Front row: Dobson, Wardley, Kemp, Young, Mehl, Thompson, Field.

Henry Anderson, mayor 1925/7, pictured here in his official robes with his wife. Mr Anderson was a reserved man, who went about his business quietly and took his civic duties in his stride. Sixty years after he retired as mayor, his two daughters, Mrs Elsie Higgins and Mrs Ethelwyne Ambrose, handed his robes over to the Dacorum Borough Council.

United States Air Force personnel stationed at Bovingdon Airfield during the Second World War, with one of their special friends, P.C. Lord.

Wings for Victory Week, May 1943. Col. Smith, US air force, taking the salute alongside the mayor, Horace Dive OBE, Alfred Marnham, Col. and Mrs Smeathman. Many organisations were included in the procession, including RAF and WAAF detachments and ATC. The Salvation Army Citadel in Marlowes is in the background.

Soldiers relaxing in Gadebridge Park, just before 1914. The soldier on the far right with his hands on his hips is Frank Middleditch.

This Isolation Hospital at Bennetts End was built in 1914 and continued as a hospital until 1981. It became a hospital for the mentally handicapped in February 1982.

William Henry Lavers, who founded a family firm of timber merchants in London in 1868. He rented a small wharf in Boxmoor in 1869 and moved to Corner Hall Wharf in 1870, where his family remain to this day. He was born in 1840 and died in 1927. The timber business is still run and owned by the Lavers family.

Three generations of the Lavers family gathered together for the Golden Wedding celebration of Mr and Mrs C.H. Lavers, c. 1945. Left to right: Mrs Elsie Lavers, Ernest W. Lavers, Hamilton Lavers, Sabina Lavers, Norman Lavers, Mary Lavers, Stewart Lavers, Mr Matthew Berry. Seated, left to right: Mrs Edith Lavers and Charles H. Lavers. Front, left to right: David Lavers, Pamela Lavers, John Lavers.

Opening ceremony of the new Corner Hall Senior school, Crabtree Lane, 1939. Earl Delaware and the mayor, Henry Fletcher, were two of the many local dignitaries who attended. Canon C.C. Hamilton is partly hidden by the mayor and Mr Barnard is on the far right.

Some of the staff at Corner Hall School, May 1949. Back row, left to right: Mr Edwards, Miss Hayden, Olive Barstow, -?-, Freda Brett. Middle row, left to right: Doris Hyde, Marjorie Fry, John Whitaker, Dora Warren, Pamela Wilkinson. Front row, left to right: Dorothy M. Tyers, Mrs Evans, Miss Jones (headmistress), Miss E.M. Badcock, Ethel Stronell.

Noake (or Noke) Mill Water End, in the days when it was used as a youth hostel, 1933/51. The site dates back to the fourteenth century and a much later building was constructed in 1850. It is now owned by Cura & Son, goldfish breeders and exotic fish importers.

Lt. Col. F.S. Brereton standing proudly outside his new car, London Road, Boxmoor. Col. Brereton had a distinguished career in the army and was made a JP and also a mayor and bailiff in 1927. He wrote many books, including *Hemel Hempstead Through the Ages*. He lived at Heath Farm (later Heath Barn) until his death in 1957 and the building now serves as a music annexe to Hemel Hempstead School.

The Bungalow, Leverstock Green Road, *c.* 1950. It was built in 1930 on land purchased from Cox Pond Farm. This was a very popular resting place for cyclists and was famous for its wonderful teas and home made ice-cream.

Ada and George Sygrave, who lived at the Bungalow and ran a catering business. They were entitled to have the C.T.C. and N.C.U. badges on the house. It was not uncommon to have as many as 100 cyclists in their garden at any one time. A third generation of Sygraves live in the bungalow today.

Parish Church of St. Mary's showing a collection of cars parked in the market square, *c.* 1947 on a no-market day. The church gates and ornamental railings have been removed, leaving only a low wall.

Gadebridge Park, before it was landscaped. The park once belonged to the Paston Cooper Estate, but was purchased by the Borough Council in 1952. The river Gade still meanders through the park and town and was popular with children for paddling and playing with boats on summer days.

Eight

Churches

St John's Church was consecrated in 1974 and built on the site of the original chapel of ease, *c.* 1829. The enlargement of 1893 can be seen in this photograph. The hedges and railings around the church have been removed and flower beds and shrubs now add to the pleasant surroundings.

The interior of St John's before considerable modernisation took place in the 1960s, which included moving the organ, creating a small meeting room and improving lighting and furnishings.

Pupils of St John's bible class outside the church parish rooms, Horsecroft Road, with their teacher, Mr Jenkins (centre). The rooms used to be used as a soup kitchen to help the poor of the parish. When St John's Hall opened in 1932, the rooms became a Working Men's Club and now serve as a thriving Social Club.

St Francis Church in Hammerfield was built in 1908. Through the generosity of Mrs Carter and others, a new church was built and opened in 1914. It is now the Church Hall.

Procession which started from the convent in Woodland Avenue making its way to St Francis Church, Hammerfield. Graham Whitlock is leading the group with the censor, followed by the Revd Derek Jackson, Peter Garner, Paul & Robert Jordan, Father E.E. Wood, the bishop of Hertford, the Rt Revd H.V. Whitsey, John Custance (head server) and the sisters of the love of God and children from the church. The special celebration was to mark the church's Diamond Jubilee, 1974.

Interior of St Mary and St Joseph in Boxmoor before enlargements and alterations took place in 1938 and 1950. The original church opened on 7 August 1898.

A new Catholic Church of St Mary the Virgin was built in St Albans Road, 1958. It developed structural problems and had to be demolished in 1987. Another church in a different style replaced it.

Wedding of Daphne Middleditch to Wally Elkins, Christ Church, 1960. George Rolph bought the site in what was Lower Cross Street, off Alexander Road, in 1879. It was the only Free Church in Hertfordshire at the time and was closed in 1973, only a few years short of its centenary.

Parish Church of St John the Baptist, Great Gaddesden. It was begun in the early twelfth century, it windows are in a fourteenth-century style, and further additions were made throughout the centuries. It contains many memorials dedicated to the Halsey family and a brick-built chapel of 1730.

St Paul's Church, Queen Street, (later Queensway). The money that went to build the church was raised by public subscription and the site given by Sir Astley Paston-Cooper. It was a chapel of ease in 1869 and a separate parish in 1878. The name of St Paul's was given to the workhouse opposite to raise its image. The church was closed in 1961 and flats built in its place.

St Paul's church choir, 1927. Back row, left to right: Lenny Evans, Alf Parrott, T (Touch'em) Sage, Harold Lavender, Nelson Seabrook, George Fells, Les Foster. Second row, left to right: Bill Sygrave, William Crook, Fred Parrott, Mr Franklin, Walter Howe, Sid Taverner, ? Tavener, ? Taverner, Mr Sage. Third row, left to right: Mr Franklin, -?- George Day, Charlie Nightingale (choirmaster), Walter East, -?-, Mr Howe, Bill Collier. Front row, left to right: Ted Parr, Mr Gibson, George Halsey, Eric Parrott, Bill Parr.

This large gathering took place on 25 March 1912. The Church of England Mission Society held a summer festival in Gadebridge, Hemel Hempstead. The day began with an organ recital in St Mary's Church and a service. Tea was held in St Mary's Hall. By the courtesy of Mr and Mrs Drake, the delegates went to the adjoining grounds of Gadebridge. There was music and games. Revd L. Gee was one of the many clergy who helped organise the day.

The newly built Wesleyan Chapel at Two Waters, Apsley, opened in February 1908. To celebrate the occasion the Trustees treated Albert Timberlake, staff and workmen to a dinner in April. The first church was a wooden hut which cost £10, known as 'Dice Box' and later, because of a flood, renamed 'Noah's Ark'. The brick building behind the new church was built in 1867 at a cost of £400.

Revd Lawrence Gee and his wife. Revd Gee was vicar at St Mary's parish church of Hemel Hempstead from 1909 to 1920.

Two of Revd Gee's children, master Willie Gee aged nine and Miss Alice Gee aged seven. These studio portraits were taken in 1920.

Was this elaborate cake made for a wedding or a special date in St Mary's Church calendar? The top tier shows a splendid model of St Mary's and the name of the church and Hemel Hempstead is written on the shield. The second tier shield says AD 1122-1927.

St Mary's is one of the oldest churches in Hertfordshire and a fine example of Norman architecture. The interior has had several changes since this shot was taken around 1902.

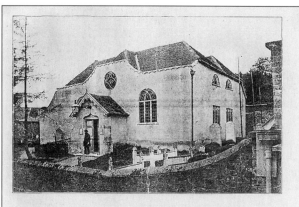

Box Lane Congregational Church.

1690—1913

A Sale of Work will be held in the Schoolroom on WEDNESDAY, September 10th.

Mrs. FORDYCE has kindly consented to open the Sale at 3 o'clock.

The Proceeds will be devoted to defraying the cost of some very necessary repairs to the roof, the walls, the gates, the notice board, and to re-colouring the walls inside the church.

Owing to the great age of the building it is imperative that it should be kept in good repair, and your interest, support and patronage are respectfully solicited.

W. WRIGHT, *Pastor.*
F. MOORE, *Treasurer.*
Mrs. CLENISTER, *Sec. Ladies' Sewing Committee.*
W. F. BOOKER, *Hon. Sec.*

Box Lane Chapel has a long history. Built in 1690, it replaced even earlier chapels and was altered in the nineteenth century when Roman remains were found. This was a poster advertising a sale of work in 1913 for financial aid for essential repairs. It closed for worship on 29 June 1969. The building is now an attractive private residence.

Interior of Box Lane chapel, just before the church furniture was taken out after closure. The clock was made by Edward Pinchbeck, 1732/66. The organ with its decorated pipes must have been a pleasing sight to the worshippers.

Members of the Box Lane Sunday school in the grounds of 'Northridge', the home of Mr and Mrs Nathaniel Micklem, where there was plenty of room for such a large gathering. The Micklam family worshipped in the chapel.

Marlowe's Baptist Church is one of the oldest Baptist Churches in the county. Members met in cottages or small buildings until the group was large enough to form their own Church. A Chapel was erected in 1700s behind Fernville Lane, which soon became too small. The group moved to the rear of the Rose & Crown, High Street. The present building opened in 1861. In October 1980 the name became Carey Church following amalgamation with Boxmoor baptist Church. It was named after William Carey, Baptist Missionary to India.

Procession of bishops and clergy for the opening ceremony of St Alban's church, Warners End, 12 October 1957. Hon. David Bowes-Lyon was present and the mayor, chairman and vice-chairman of the development corporation.

Church of St Alban's on its opening day, 1957. The foundation stone had been laid the previous October and blessed by the bishop of St Alban's. A wooden hut had been set up as a temporary measure before the church was built. The priest-in-charge, Revd K.D. Greenaway had been working in the district since 1954. The church was designed by Mr H. Kellett Ablett FRIBA, chief architect in the development corporation.

Nine

Freetime

Wagonette outing, or maybe a wedding party, *c.* 1908. Several of the people are in their best clothes and wearing buttonholes.

Members of Boxmoor Cricket Club, 1957.

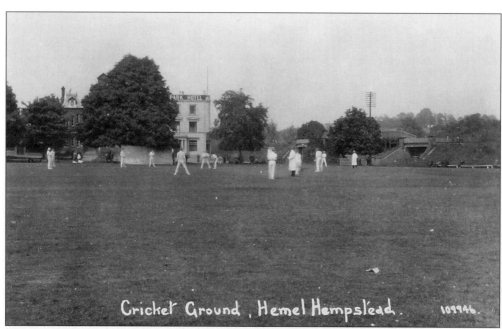

Cricket Ground, Hemel Hempstead.   109946.

Hemel Hempstead cricket ground situated by Heath Park Hotel and Heath Park Halt. The railway bridges are in the background and the roads led to the town and to Two Waters. Heath Park Hotel has since undergone rebuilding and a recent change of name.

The Golf Links, Boxmoor

Boxmoor golf links were established over 100 years ago. Since this photograph was taken in the 1920s, many of the surrounding trees have matured considerably.

Central School cycle run, 1937. The children and teachers pause for a photograph on the main road by the moor.

Boxmoor ramblers football team, 1913/14. Only one name is known: Joseph Fairbank, who had a newsagents and sweet shop in St John's Road, Boxmoor.

Churchill outdoor pool, 1957. The pool was so popular, it was hard to find a space on the grass for sunbathing in between swims. The season ran from 1 May to September and in the early days the pool was unheated.

The Debonaires Dance Band were formed in 1947. They played at Watford Town Hall for many years and in London Hotels. In 1948 they were *Melody Maker* Champions and runners up the following year. Bill Lee was on piano, Chick Chapel on clarinet, Ron Oldham on drums, Bert Lambert on string bass, Percy Stevens on alto sax, Bob Thompson the first alto, Jerry Ayres on guitar, George Bennett on tenor sax, Fred Gurney on trombone, George Scarff first trumpet, Ken Tearle second trumpet. Most of the members worked at John Dickinson's.

Third Boxmoor Scout troop, 1915, with their scoutmaster, E.H. Lidderdale, who was affectionatley known as 'Nunc'.

Gym display by the third Boxmoor troop of boy scouts, as they were known in the '30s. In the grounds of scoutmaster E.H. Lidderdale's house 'Boisden'. The top floor of the building was fitted out as a den and a workshop and was a place where scouts could play games and study for badges.

110

Was this a first-aid class demonstrating folding arm slings, or a dance using scarves for visual effect? Whatever it was, it seemed to be a serious matter. The photograph dates from *c.* 1900.

Marlowe's baptist and methodist tennis club, Fernville Lane, *c.* 1937. Back row, left to right: Gurney, -?-, -?-, Jim Ripman, -?-, -?-, -?-, -?-, Cyril Taylor, Jimmy Waterhouse, Harold Simmonds. Front row, left to right: Freda Mark, -?-, Phyllis Jennings, Peggy Pollard, -?-, Nancy Mark, Ethel Simmonds, Barbara Simmonds, -?-. Mascot unknown.

Shendish Day, 1968. John Dickinson employees and their children being entertained by a Punch and Judy man at Apsley Mills Sports Centre. Shendish House belonged to the Longman family until John Dickinson's bought it for their employees in 1937 and made it into a sports and social club.

Tug of war team, 1929. Standing near Harding's Bridge. The trophy was the Apsley Challenge Cup. Members were presented with biscuit barrels as souvenirs of the occasion.

Hemel Hempstead Athletic Club, 1908/9. The back of the postcard reads, '5 mile race has been postponed, will not take place tomorrow. Will advise later.' It is written by F. Harding Hon. Sec. and addressed to R. Halsey, Brydens Camp, Water End, H.H.

Members of the Hemel Hempstead Amateur Operatic and Dramatic Society performing 'Breath of Spring', 1961. Muriel Kench, Sheila Charge, Bill Davies, May Greenaway and Sonia Sully. The society was formed in 1925.

John Dickinson Band, c. 1963. Back row, left to right: J. Langford, R. Hill, T. Goodman, J. Eddon, E. Phelps, W. Briggs, D. Wells, H. Cook, M. Hydon, P. Gibbs, D. Savill. Middle row, left to right: H. Evans, P. Davis, H. Austin, B. Boarder, W. Gurney, J. Dimes, H. Thompson, F. Gurney, T. McGuire, K. Spillett. Front row, left to right: R. Hampton, H. Burgess, E. Cleveland, D. Howe (bandmaster), R. Burgess (secretary), G. Brand (conductor), R. Seabrook, S. Devlin, R. Oldham. The photograph was taken in the guildhouse, Apsley, with some of the cups and trophies won that year.

Ten
Special Days

Photograph by local photographer Culverhouse. Group dressed up as playing cards.

The celebrations at Apsley and Nash Mills for George V's Coronation in 1911 lasted twelve hours and ended with a torchlight procession and fireworks.

Souvenir programme to celebrate King George V's coronation in 1911. Events began with a church parade and thanksgiving service in St Mary's at 10 a.m. followed by races for children and dinner for the widows and the aged. The day ended at 10 p.m. with a bonfire and rockets on Roughdown common.

116

Main London Road, Apsley, 1911. All the decorations are up and the children are waiting for the day's festivities to begin. St Mary's church dominates the skyline and next to it was the Salmon Pub. Apsley Working Men's Club is the large building on the right, hardly recognisable under all the decorations.

Empire Day, 1913. The streets of Apsley were filled with people and decorated floats for this special day in May. Shop signs advertising Cadbury's chocolates and Lyons Tea are still with us today. Kent's brush factory chimney is also advertising their product of high quality brushes.

Another horse and cart beautifully decorated and waiting to join a procession. People on the float look very happy depicting a wedding. St Mary's church is in the background. The photograph was taken by F. Palmer of Ebberns Road, Apsley.

The Jolly Organ Boys, c. 1920 used to dress up for the annual rag appeal to raise funds for Hemel Hempstead Hospital. They gave many hours of their time to help this worthy cause.

The 1922 Pageant involved many people of the town, including Miss Mary Dale and her brothers Alfred (seated) and William Dale who took the role as the King's falconer.

Lockers Park was the perfect setting for the Boxmoor Pageant, held in July 1922. Much money was raised by this event for Boxmoor St John's new hall. The period costumes everyone wore and the story of Hemel Hempstead's history was an occasion to remember for many years.

Apsley Cycling Club, July 1906, when everyone wore hats! Some of the people are known, including Arthur Allum, Jimmy Hall, Bill Green, Jack Wills, Doug Smith, Billy Butler, Bill Porter, Bill Coker, Dick Scrivener, Bert Welling, Arthur Simpson, Jim Sparrow, Harry Palmer. Bill Turvey is sitting front right and George Attaway front left. None of the ladies' names are known.

Wedding photograph of Mr and Mrs Cecil Chennells, 1 January, 1911. The maiden name of Mrs Chennells was Ada Maggie Bennett. Mr and Mrs Chennells both lived well into their nineties. Mr Chennells was a local postman for forty years and a keen gardener.

Wedding group of Gladys Wheeler and Frank Rolph, 1928. The wedding took place at St John's Church and the reception was held at St Francis, Hammerfield.

This Leyland Club fire engine was put to a different use the day it was required to take Doris Allen and Ralph Tomkins to their reception after their wedding. The bridesmaid is L. Allen. Among those of the firemen from the Apsley Brigade were CO A. Jones, J. Lee, Ted Cripps and L. Dorrofield. The building in the background is the parish rooms.

Souvenir Programme
~~~~

Children's Party

GIVEN BY THE
RESIDENTS OF

Deaconsfield Rd.

TO   CELEBRATE

V.E. & V.J. Days

Souvenir programme of V.E. and V.J. Day
celebrations. A party was held at Crabtree School.
Sports and races were followed by tea, a cinema
show and conjuring act, ending with a bonfire and
fireworks.

Boxmoor guides celebrating V.E. Day 1945 by picnicing in the field behind the Poplars, Cowper
Road.

One of the many street parties held to celebrate the end of the Second World War. 'Down the Dip' in the High Street, Hemel Hempstead, 1945.

Group of Girls and Boys Life Brigade outside St Albans Church, Warners End, 1950s. The Girls Life Brigade was established in 1902 by the Sunday School Union in the City of London to provide weekly night activity that would keep girls in close touch with the church and Sunday school. Lt. M. Greenaway is on the far left.

7th Battalion Hertfordshire Home Guard, No 2 Platoon (Boxmoor). A social evening was held at St John's Hall on 5 May 1945. Platoon roll, January 1944: Lt. H.T. King, Lt. J.W.Thorne, Plt. Sgt. K. Waterton, Sgt. R. Prince, A.E. Glover, F. Cristall, F.G. Doggett, C.L. Dunham, B.J. Jolliffe, Cpl. R. Earle, A. Woodford, E.J. Akers, Lovesay, J. King, A. Rowe, I. Hamer, H.O. Ormes, W. Reynolds, L/Cpl. A. Bates, L. Thorne, E. Newcombe, P. Hopcroft, A. Batchelor, D. Johnson, H. Allen, A.G. Bedford, H. Barber, E.E. Barber, H.T. Bates, E. Baker, H. Bisney, C. Burnham, E. Branch, A.E. Cox, J.W. Carlette, A. Cheshire, J. Critchely,

A. Charge, W. Charge, D. Clarke, A.W. Dell, W. Dawkins, F.A. Dunham, H.G. Element, F. Finch, E.C. Fielding, A.J. Gower, L. Gower, R. Herbert, A. Hemly, R.A. Hoar, G. Harrison, W. J. Jones, B.D. Jay, H. Langdale, J. Lee, E.E. Leeds, H.M. Latchford, A. Myatt, W.G. McDonald, N.K. McDonald, J. Milne, T.G. Mabey, A. Maydom, R.C. Norrie, J. Palmer, G. Paiba, H. Rubins, W. Randell, G.J. Rogers, J. Ranscombe, F. Simms, W. Sander, D. Saunders, A.B. Sharp, F.J. Shouler, H. Stannard, J. Tipping, H. Talbot, K. Walker, M.J. Watchorn, E.H. Woods, J.M. Williams.

Queens Square, July 20, 1952. Members of the British Legion and other organisations waiting to welcome Her Majesty the Queen Elizabeth, visiting Hemel Hempstead to lay the Foundation Stone of St Barnabus Church. The platform where the ceremony was to take place is on the far right of the picture.

Vicar of Hemel Hempstead, Revd Canon C.H. Plummer, escorted Princess Margaret when she visited the town on 6 April 1961 to meet young church goers at Highfield and representatives of the other area churches, St Pauls, St Albans, St Peters, St Barnabus, St Stephens, and All Saints. Lts. Day and Smale, Lance cpl. Wright and Carter were present and the captain of the GLB was presented to HRH.

Hemel Hempstead Cycling Club held a dinner for their members and the winners were presented with cups and trophies, 1957/8. S. Hall, W. Byrne, R. Macey and J. Stewart are pictured here. Mr Syd Goodwin, the president and founder member, presided.

Garden fete display held in the grounds of St Nicholas by the Girl's Life Brigade, 1957. All the children were asked to wear white blouses, tea-shirts and coloured cotton skirts for dancing.

Supper in honour of the Hemel Hempstead Amateur Operatic and Dramatic Society held in St John's Hall, February 21, 1933, in the presence of the mayor and mayoress of Hemel Hempstead. The menu comprised clear soup, lobster patties, cold turkey, sausage and ham, potatoes, trifle, cheese, rolls, lemonade, cider and beer.

The 21st birthday of the Townswomen's Guild, formed in May 1941, celebrated by an evening of entertainment at St John's Hall, May 1962. Present were May Greenaway (as Mary Queen of Scots), Dorothy Smale, Margaret West, Gladys Oakins, Ethel Reynolds and Nita Woodman.